A Place Made Fast

Mark Halperin

A Place Made Fast

Copper Canyon Press

Acknowledgments

Versions of some of these poems appeared in the following magazines: *Agenda* (England), *Carolina Quarterly, Choomia, Backdoor, Chowder Review, Epoch, Iowa Review, Jeopardy, New Letters, Pearl* (Denmark), *Poetry, Poetry Northwest, Poetry NOW, Porch, Quarterly West, Shenandoah, Sonora Review, Southern Poetry Review, Vagabond, Virginia Quarterly Review, Whetstone, Willow Springs.*

In slightly altered form and with the exception of "Fasting On Yom Kippur" and "For My Birthday," all the poems in section II were published in THE WHITE COVERLET, in Jawbone Press' chapbook series (Seattle, 1979).

"Gomer" was published in a limited edition by SeaPen Press and Papermill (Seattle, 1979).

"Paul Celan" appeared as part of PASSWORDS, an anthology printed in a limited edition by SeaPen Press and Papermill (Seattle, 1979).

"Franz Jagesttater's Epistemology" appeared in THE POET'S CHOICE, an anthology published by Tendril Press (Boston, 1980).

The author was aided in completing this manuscript by a Faculty Summer Research Grant for which he is grateful to Central Washington University.

Publication of this book was made possible in part by grants from the Washington State Arts Commission and the National Endowment for the Arts. Thanks also to Centrum, where Copper Canyon is press-in-residence.

Copper Canyon Press, P.O. Box 271, Port Townsend, Washington 98368

FOR B

CONTENTS

One

A SERVANT

One day he could not keep his hands
from the fine china he brought the king.
He saw a white snake in a white bowl
and ate. After that, he could hear animals
talking like men. The fish he put back

in water, the ants he stepped around,
and for the fledgling ravens who had fallen
from their nest, he killed his own horse,
cutting the flesh into strips they could eat.
Aided by the fish, the ants, and the ravens,

he completed the assigned tasks and married
the princess. Then he was glad of the golden apple
whose magic could transform her hatred
into love and relieve him from the life
that once a man was born to. Still,

in this strict economy, the trade of good
for good had left his first betrayal:
and there was the dead horse he must have heard
begging for its life, a servant as he had been.
Now, though he is a king, he cannot bear

to let others remove his uneaten food.
He tells them stories of his first country
where the chirping of birds was only music.

TWO LINES FROM PAUL CELAN

At nightfall the sky was various
blues and grays moving into each other.
You drew the drapes then gathered
with the others before the wireless,
only you listening to the leaves
fill like teacups. Then the war was over

and you lived in this foreign city
where you have slipped on a raincoat
and gone for the evening paper.
Behind a warehouse, the yellow moon
rises, bearing your lost mittens
and the copybook between whose ruled veins

you had seen the sky at Gilgal
keeping light wonderfully, a drama
of finite scope, finite duration.
The next day, your parents packed
an overnight bag. Smoke
widens at the tall brick stacks

east of you. They never returned.
The boy who dashes past bends
his head, but you have seen his eyes,
blue or brown as your own. You lift
your collar and cross one of the bridges,
pass beneath the streetlamps, from light

to dark, from dark to light,
to your own door. You've forgotten
the paper, but the mittens are
recollected and, safely, the copybook too.
At your back, leaves turn over. The wind
spills them carrying a Russian song.

The sun stood still; the moon halted.
A circus? the seacoast? Out of what
other contradiction could you hope
to render such implacable grief:
things lost were not lost,
the heart was a place made fast.

KITTITAS HORSES

From far off we heard the din
of trampling horses and howling dogs
and by noon were seeking the camp's center,
a coolness of children through which we moved
cautiously, not to breach
their etiquette. And that night
the braves went about stealing our horses,

our kettles
no sooner on the fire
than five or six spears bore off their contents.
The next day, by luck or grace,
I thought to fetch a paper-cased looking glass
and a little vermillion to
Eyacktana, their chief, with whom I criss-crossed the camp
as he shouted, *deliver up the horses*

and more softly, *I have spoken well in your favor*,
snatching the beads as fast I fished them up,
two buttons, then two rings. My fear
had long since passed into lassitude.

I told myself, I am reading a book
with marbled covers: two men, both white, meet.
The first cradles a rifle. Under a huge cliff
of brow, his eyes are black, blank
until the second, who resembles me,
mounted, comes abreast.
When the horse passes, he drops
to one knee

and fires. I was free
to pay the toll of my disposition: not axes
for beaver pelt or horses
but our lives in my impossible calculations,

my refuge. I see Eyacktana
grabbing the knife of one of my Canadians,
the man, enraged, making toward him—
for a longer time, Indians chinking the gaps.

*Here my friend
is a chief's knife,* I said, with no guess
what he might do, no book the outcome hidden
only by dirtied paper. Eyacktana
held it aloft as he would hold the pipe

and at that moment
was no more mysterious than my own kind
in the settlement or the man in the story,
gratuitous as all of these exchanges:
the eighty-five Kittitas horses I got, the presents
of Eyacktana also, two horses, twelve beaver,

dark, luxurious pelts. I sent
my men off then, but before I left, gave away
my belt, my hat and pipe.
Then their women brought a variety of eatables
which I ate, hungrily,
like a man who has just passed
through a great danger
or one who has become its prisoner.

IN THE NINETEENTH CENTURY

for Barbara Anderson

In the Nineteenth Century everything
was hazy. The heads of oaks about to burst
into flame, the heart-shaped leaves
of lindens trapped the mist
above ponds and wreathed lakes—
fog would cling

to any water that moved.
The faces of couples who strolled
the wharves blurred. A woman's hair
was a nimbus, each fold of cloth
soft. Above the tow-paths,
high and thinned, clouds

banked. *The lover gives away
his will*, a boy swore
as a countess would. They were all rich,
neurasthenic, pale
or belligerent peasants

who stooped at shovels, drew
lines and manned the streets. That last day
shadows crisped on the villa walls
and garbage stank. A horse
lay down in a ditch
and no one could recall what passion meant.

VOLTAIRINE DE CLEYRE AT ST. JOHNS

It is December, the prairie broad and buried;
last night I saw the moon on all that white.

There must be nothing in me to slow the flood—
even the black dog that sat down by me
in Brooks Street comes back:
how he wanted to lie in my lap,
how I carried him upstairs,

the awful gulp when he stiffened.

And the little Sister who kissed me
when the others frowned—she has a piece
I wrote for her and sometimes reads it over.

I judge my life wretched
but the Haymarket comrades
who bowed to no God,
believed in no hereafter
went triumphantly to the gallows. So

I walk about and dust as I promised,
three snubs of lead in me.
The poor boy who fired them
did less harm than my body, at forty-three

so weak I hear a roaring train
passing a window, but inside
my head, as in an empty hall.

When I stopped in Port Huron on my way here
it seemed the mill had gone backward: discouraged
piles of lumber leaning and rank weeds

to the rotting backwater.
The old convent is sold for apartments.

Mother is sure to be miserable once I pack.

Berckman has written: his book does not go.
I have answered, lie on the grass,
watch the ants—let the sun burn
into you day after day
until the thoughts fill you again;
but I fail to convince myself.

I get hold of a thought. In a few days
it appears foolish.
Then another crops up, then it goes smash.

Ten yards from the window
a rabbit lifts its head. Now
the man hears the dog too—
a spot of white disappearing.
He pushes his chair back. He's
pulled down a sheaf of drawings
and hunts through details of porticos
and lintels for a shot-window.

A tomcat purrs. Snow keeps falling.
Two women, one alive, one dead,
lie in their separate cold beds.
The primroses of April: that window
can return them. And grass
will wave under his pencil
again, under the window. As a carriage
nears, the rabbit will go on

eating fresh shoots, undisturbed
because a carriage is neither
man nor dog. That shot-window,
if he could find it, would rescue
a memory, nothing lodged behind it.
The cat's paws flex. The man
slips one sheet over the next,
lamplight flickering like snow.

As they argued, the bishop had yelled, *arrogant
man*, furious with Jagesttater, who is mounting steps
smoothed by the passage of others. In the courtyard
a swath of light brushes his shoulder. Why
is Berlin so much colder than his Austrian village,
its bluebells and edelweiss? In 1943

the ageless Church holds it is wrong, knowingly,
to serve in an unjust war. Jagesttater's wife,
shifting her chair closer to the fire, hears the cat
yawn who is sleeping where her husband should be
reading to her of oil and grain in the godless east.
Jagesttater's rosary is his single argument: God

gave us reason and meant us to distinguish
good from evil. This is not a man to consider
how long it takes the brain to die and feeling
to shut down, but Jagesttater, shuffling
toward the dark wooden block. He believes in God
and the Holy Catholic Church; he knows this war

is unjust, and trusts his legs will not buckle.
It is sad to die, although belief and trust abide
like the sun clearing the Alps, casting the shadow
of a cross over the play of his small children.
Poor orphans, he permits himself; his gift: belief
in a loving God, and his certainty: *men may know*.

How even the light is on this afternoon
of my fifth year. Mother must hear
the radio, she pushes the vacuum
through such graceful arabesques.
I am not paying attention to my cards

but to Mother, beautiful in her short skirt
and cream blouse, light shining
in the edges of her upswept hair.
We are home alone, sharing the room
while we do our work. Mother has made a turn

toward the kitchen. She switches
the machine off, sinking to the rug.
On the radio a man is repeating the hour
the President died. Mother sobs
but she has remembered to open her arms

and I have climbed in them, my cheek
on her breast. I tell her not to
but she cries. There is music,
very slow and not to dance to, and Mother
rocking me in that bright room.

Two

IN THE OLD DAYS

scarlet fever and whooping cough stooped
low at the lintels like messengers from a king,

and when they entered, child followed child
into the ground, still clutching a parent's

long face, gnawing hollows in the cheeks.
Mother left thoughts of heaven to others

wiser than herself, but she imagined hell
down to the blinking nails and heat that rose

in sheets, unrolled to the corners and swelled
like bells or bread. Snow drifted, fell deep.

Scabs peeled, exposing the unmarked skin
of the child who coughed in his sleep. Father

climbed his moaning wife and when her head twisted
toward the wall, tightening, he spurted

the ghostlike drops. They'd sigh. Sometimes
they'd forget, tumbling toward some lake's

unruffled surface. In the dark a wind
blew up out of the south. *Mother, Father . . .*

Small voices called, the icicles, that roof
of fringes, tinkling before each stabbed the ground.

MY FATHER'S DEATH

1.

I'm helping a friend move in a slow truck
fifty miles, the windshield shrunk
by ice to a peephole. We cross
the black Columbia. Waxy stars
ignite. We unload boxes
of books, of crated tools, and before the lock
is snapped, step back. Sprawled before us,
the shed is a wreckage of snow, crust
and soft underbelly lit by the moon.

On the way back, we search for the center line,
hunched forward, cold as the stove
in the house he's emptied and means to leave.
I leave him there, drive toward the dogs,
a child, and my wife who talks
carefully, awkward with the news. I phone.
My mother sobs. The walls of the house
whiten, break in—
I stand, as before my father, a son.

2.

Morning through afternoon I'd sat
at your bedside, your heart "strong as a bull,"
your eyes a refugee's, drained and set.
The hand I rubbed would pull
away. You'd whisper, *Please, Boris,*
Sonya, they're killing me. They were, we were,
but not in Odessa where the postman's sightless horse

dragged you through flames, and the arms that wrapped yo
were yours, your family sustained
through seventy years. I forced you back
to bed, that wild look drained.
After I left, you fought them.
You'd swing till you cleared a path
past the doctors, the nursing home, unfair,

and labored on less and less.
You were down to ninety pounds, but strong
enough to be dangerous.
I think of your wife, as you intended,
asleep. She never heard a sound
when at home, in your own bed, finally it ended.

-3.

I ski a hard six miles up
and stop to catch my breath:
the first or next day. Unable
to rest or let go, I edge

toward your absence where
words I can't say honor you
in hiding, the shy bridegroom,
tense, licking and liking
the salt of reticence. Day

nine or two: I go for firewood
and talk around the backs of
stumps, blackish or brown, shattered
but cordial while they hold you
off. Whatever will fall

like a bead of melt or drops
like a cold coin to my hand
I draw back from. This is
the day that has no number,
the veiled one, the widow.

SAL

The people we knew for years on Jewel Avenue
and a Hundred and Forty-seventh Street
all left home. Ashes in the lee
of a big boat kicking up sheets,
the spume that fogs the Inland Waterway
on a terrace south of there.
Seventeenth Street, where you could write your name
in soot and leave a bare
trace like snow. It boils up. Salvador
La Placa, where are you? Where's your uncle's
radio that played in the Hudson Tubes?
For all I know you've been back,
but I doubt it. The brick and mortar
of our two-story houses could be dust

for all the difference it makes.
Snow covers someone else's farm
or dowdy suburb land—
white knuckled hands out of the past.
It's started again. I used to think
we'd meet over a couple of beers. I'd have learned
to leave well enough alone.
Six months, almost two thousand miles
to the south, I answer myself. No snow here.
Sal, you can find my mother, my sister
or I can. I can't find my father.
Those arches we pissed at the garage door
were perfect, one friendship I won't know.

Two weeks into April, buds on the currants
swell; snow; the ants crawl indoors.
I remember your writing to me, in secret once:
I miss the seasons. The square of spotty grass,
maples, the vacant lot where you'd walked
some dog for thirty years, they ached
in you. You told me nothing lasts,

or I imagine it was you who could pretend
only a date had to be fixed
and I'd be on your terrace, drink in hand,
making small talk or eating breakfast—
and visits after that. The wind is up.
In every room doors rattle.
The wild rose thrashes a windowsill.

In spring, a cloudless night, I walk outside
lashed by my own hair, in tow
and listening to the river roar, muddied,
swollen, burdened by run-off. A widow
calls each Sunday to tell me she's doing fine.
The habits last, not the loss, treeless vistas
and these letters I send that cannot arrive.

The dead woman's child is quiet.
Shadows divide us. Who her mother was fond of,
how she cocked her head listening—our speech
thickens like first ice on a pond.
The day cools as we sit with a funeral
more recent than my father's. His descends,
the colors of sunset, thinner, less.

Behind stacks of themselves,
walls of themselves, heaped up
on each other like logs, they break,
are sucked back to rock in their deep
troughs, which is how we lose them.

My farmer friend was puzzled
in the shade. His visitors hadn't changed
so he couldn't keep them.
Between the orange backhoe and sky-blue hives
hung death and my fear of it.
Our lives should lead us
past that, he said, then talked on.

Don't run over that dead bird
or he will be *very angry*, my son
tells me, and I swerve as I would have
without his warning. Is it alarm
at the shiny guts, the feathers?
Do they feel
or wait for him like the cups he spills?

Weeks pass when I don't love myself.
My hands dangle. Nothing can touch
the bit of granite where I rock.
How do I reach
my father? He droops from lack of attention

like newly set out vines. The heat.
His memory thirsts for me or I for him.

Of course we are the dead, not just
their spokesmen, but their genitals
convulsing, their arms, their damp skin,
the hair, the teeth. When we lose ourselves
they push us back into these bodies,
Draco, Orion, so far away
it's frightening, when we try to count them, so many.

I'm from the mountains. By the sea
a few days, I'm almost in love
or am, am married, single. At lunch
she bares her foot. When she walks off
for good, I don't try to follow.
There are no keepsakes
of what goes, and everything does.

We left them—or they left us—coarser.
Our skin is ridged and thickens
under our fingers.

FROM A FILE

It must be evening there, the sky
full of clouds like those in Hokusai's
Red Fuji, windrows drawn by an accomplished hand.
By now he must be stirring, blear eyed
and dull, the infant making for his lap.

Something's hushed about this scene
in which his wife sniffs meat and slices peppers
into neat strips, the rows like three women
who stride toward the white corner of the t.v.
Called to, the man lifts his head, and perhaps

from a file in which the past is kept,
some cruelty of a father lights like a fly
on his plate. He slumps in the chair again, falls
through himself and the whitening bodies
of his loves, the arms of friendship, even

through his own child's need.
Trees watch him. Each place he travels to,
clouds draw gauze around his breathing
and sand slips open to receive him.
Someone shouts through cupped hands.

And still you make your unexpected visits
like the whiskered, rheumy-eyed old men
in ear-curls who collected alms for *Eretz
Yisrael*. They wouldn't come in.
They stood on the step and held out cans that itched
for our small coins. After they'd left
garlic lingered with the sing-song Yiddish
in which flowers are violets
or roses, or have no names. Did Holy Soil
for graves run out? the neighborhood too Gentile
for them? I've forgotten.

I'm a continent away. One afternoon
it all comes back. I watch the hawk
on the telephone pole and try to drive home
his whites and browns. When I look up
I sit for a while, Father, in such repose
you seem to have joined me. As the light fades
my child babbles on till his Momma knows
something landed. We choose
little enough. How could I lose you?

FASTING ON YOM KIPPUR

Today the pear trees wrapped in shawls of air,
the wind that bends them booming with frogs—

but I am not wearing a new blue suit. My hair
is not perfumed spikes of black that poke out

under a white skull-cap. This day each year
the Law added our sins to our father's.

All the Jewish boys were absolved
like trees that drop their foliage

all at once. We'd play at prayer and fasting,
at emptying and the chest-thumping of grown men

till sundown. A few remaining leaves scratch
and their dry cough recalls the drone

of men in prayershawls, the tinkle of glasses
later, a table heaped with herring and sardines.

My heart catches. Netted, it bangs
louder. We stiffen, our yearly rings

unbreathable armor without forgetfulness.
Without memory we repeat our fathers, slip

and vanish around the trunks of pear trees.
I fast today. I walk out past

the unpruned orchard,
nostalgia's branches clacking.

FOR MY BIRTHDAY

The child who tugs my arm toward faded marigolds
    stoops as I crush a flower. I spread
its seeds across my palm: they're hair-like,

half dark and barbed. And he looks at each before
    he lets it slip into the envelope.
He fingers the flap almost as I touched the bones

in my face this morning. When he looks up, he wants
    to see the seeds a second time. I pinch
the envelope open. *It's my birthday*, I tell him,

pull at tall weeds. The wind scatters his hair. Before
    we reach the backdoor, he's grabbing
what's closest, his puffy hands emptying and closing on mine.

VISITING

... honest courage and myself in my army, I led the
way and my troops soon followed.
          John Clare on the third day to Northborough

Maybe once in two years I'm with a friend.
Sitting by the door, I watch his cheeks
puff out and flex, his lounging heart.
The other guests arrive and the talk
starts hard. His daughter,
coiling pink embroidery
at her throat, cries because she's just plain cold,
and tired of the open mouths of visitors,
she follows the floor and lighted hall to bed.

As for Clare's bizarre invention,
it bridged the way toward hope but was
too thin to bear him any happiness,
his choice, be sane or eat. History
was cruel. The actual man
could choose less.
Infrequently returning, the visits each predictable,
he shudders for what's to come. And when I visit
you, who's to say which of us is bereft?

The bald hill I climbed with friends,
from which I saw the river wind through a half circle
of trees—we got chased away by yellow jackets,
the shrieking girl stirring a ground nest
that swarmed and stung us all.
We hadn't enough time for our hands
to come down. Now you are all gone.
The present is brief
as mad John Clare would understand.

PLAYING WITH THE CHILDREN

for Deanna and John Rengstorff

We meant to bring a patriarch
or wildflower home,
so when the children were born
we gave them those names. And rocked
and waded the winter's several darks
cradling armfuls whose languages
dimmed. It was like a memory of steerage.
Noah commanding the dogs to bark,
Alyssa gathering lavender—
we were their innocents,
arms open at first steps;
they only mimicked our passing gestures.

Histories would vanish that hadn't formed
in the half-light of the morning
and we could begin
over and lighter, but the children performed
miracles, retrieving a word,
an intimidating finger
until they trapped us. An eye flickered.
We took it for love, then gave away
more, until into us
their laughter fell like snow
descending all afternoon on a bay.

AFTER THE HAILSTORM

I wish I'd made my son a human song
to hold like a hand with the odor
and light of his mother's hair,
till he dozed. The dark wants us and must belong

where we live, it finds us so often.
I'm in the next room where
the fire roars. His bears,
beside him, already sleep. The dark of the sky

belongs to the night, not the afternoon storm
when thunder clapped and hail
filled his blue cup
with perfect ice balls. Each was a fairy tale.

In one, a ragged flock of magpies
flashed just long enough
to rise, smoke-puffs.
It was a picture someone would notice only once.

In another his hair flew. And colder,
altered by the years, in the last
his face was dry.
In the morning we will both wake older.

Three

TROTSKY ON EXILE

1.

In the depot, when the train halts
twelve unexplained days, I watch
a pile of empty tins rise from the snow,
a metal tree like the lamps of a reading room,
each book constructing the earnest future.
Thus my exile begins as a trial
forced to think its way backwards.

We have been switched onto the wrong siding,
I nurse that insane hope until the miles
dissolve—Odessa, Constantinople,
Prinkipo's ramshackle villa.

Mornings I pull at the oars of a battered skiff,
toss stones where my Greek friend directs.
When the net fills we haul in, but argue
in such a polyglot, my letters
seem lobsters climbing from the pail
into air they can't breathe.

I think, a sea and centuries away
in Rome any sentence of death
could be exchanged for exile.

The crates jammed with carbons and clippings
travel with me, but the past, all the same,
disappears in my wake: Zimmerwald,
Alma-Ata, Barbison. The news catches up with us
in Rivera's Blue House: Sedov is murdered.

Natalia and I keep sequestered five welcome days.

How does one accept a land
or grief, belong to those fictions of scale

when all about swarm others who live
and die at home, calmly absorbed
in the familiar view from a window?

2.

Papery fronds flap along the far wall
of Coyouacan's Avenida Viena while the guard
enters a shadow turquoise as the Mediterranean,
other worlds though no older than this one.

When Captain Salazar approaches, I bury
my fingers in the soft ears of a rabbit.
We eat these, I answer his doubts:
seventy bullet holes and no one seriously injured.
I point to the rows of hutches, swaying

as if I'd stepped from a locomotive,
it's German steam, and bellowed *stern measures!*
I recall Lenin, sick, uncontrollably angered
at butter in the Kremlin. *Who is to blame?*
This one asks too. Seventy bullet holes
and only Seva, little Seva has bloodied his toe.

But Zinaida, Sergi, Sedov lie dead. My children.
Who is to blame? When I answer, Joseph Stalin,

it is a joke

only in part, as I have been a revolutionary
forty-four years, how many outside exile?
I lift the limp rabbit inside his house.
Bright green grass beneath the wall,
sunlight everywhere. When our histories
assume a studied casualness, we know better.

At the materializing seance thirty-one spirits
paraded from my cabinet, Captain Hodges,
Alice, Little Wolf and Tom Higgens, they tell me,
who, a-hunting, called to his dog
and took frequent tugs from his whiskey. The audience
was rough looking scoffers. I remember

the light in a pine forest, so deep
a green it seemed liquid. My pleasure
recalling it is womanish; there was no pleasure
then. Other children
played at hiding
behind the watering trough. In the isolation
of my sickbed their heard laughter
tinkled like icicles an hour after dawn.

Unhappiness that great
requires some gift, and illness
was mine. When tortures had abraded
the material covering my soul,

and it shone through,

I was too surprised to wonder, but strained
at footsteps beyond the fence's palings,
the voices of strolling
couples, only
intended for me. Of course

I am being used. We all are—how marvelously
is the only test. Callused hands press
my body when I can reach no voice,
but are satisfied
with the silk that encumbers my flesh. The subtler
fluid eludes them. Once

being forbidden to climb aboard Papa's favorite mare,
I knotted my hands
in her coarse mane and galloped a half mile.
She dumped me, roaring on
then coming back through the dust the other way.
The night I discovered my gift

I also cried. I still do
though that is *one* side as this life is
only the one on this side. And last night
the audience cheered when I finished.

One bull-chested man, with the heckler's
twisted brow, grabbed the few he considered
too slow and set them on their feet
like tin soldiers. His wet cheeks glistened.
In the street the stars rang
with a happiness I knew
was borne aloft by conviction.

GOMER

So he went and took Gomer, a worthless woman.
THE BOOK OF HOSEA

1.

My sisters and I were girls, younger anyway
and for a while no one noticed what we wore.
We tried on the maid's dress, Papa's chapped
and chalky shoes.
Behind the outbuildings
whose silvered wood splintered when we rubbed it

our bodies were simply bodies
and perfect blankets to sleep in
and the hair on them, so light it seemed
the tongue of a flame danced behind.
Then the first dark ones sprouted.
Though none hurt, they were worse

than teeth coming in. Not that we hadn't been
yelled at for not washing, preferring our dolls
to the stern, *stand, eat, sleep.* Still,
those commands were simple and I could tell
from the sensible if pinched eyes of my mother

now there was a manner that followed
the summons of breasts. The skill to keep back
a look of interest—when no one
was home, we sneaked into our rooms
to talk, good slaves,
guessing a wish before the words formed.

2.

So Hosea came to my father, counting out
the money and wheat while I stood outside
with the only virtue left, not to hurt
anyone. And he was no longer the boy
I'd peeped at from the curtains, a full head
lower than I, half expecting him to pee.

I rubbed my sore chest against the archway,
measured him: not as broad as my father,
not glaring as Father glared. Raw hands

smoothed his hair back, counting the jars
of new wine. When told
I went to him who had bought me, hands
thick enough to rub the skin off a girl's arm.
I went, told to

by my father, as my sisters, swept off
for no apparent reason, because what else
is there to do? He brushed the hair
between my legs, not even a moan.

Then I knew he'd handed over the coins
slowly, not because they were hard
to part with or he doubted my value;
numbers were difficult work for such a one,

unlike walking all day behind the dirty backs
of oxen. What could I wait for
beside a child? I draw fresh water.

While he goes on sleeping, I place a bowl
and spoon on the worn boards of the table.
I sit on a stool. After he is up,
I will be alone, disguised like this
though he leaves me here by myself all day.

3.

Once clouds rolled down from Golan.
I rushed out with an oilskin and saw him
stock still behind the plow. Does he talk
to Baal, the One we're not supposed to?
When he tramped back, it was more than mud;
his anger, as if he were cursing his wife

and a little fleshy nob instead of a stomach,
a nameless disease. Pleased enough

it was a boy, naming it Jezreel, "God Shall Sow,"
he loved to stand above the crib, swinging
one finger left, right, watching
the child's monotonous eyes follow,
letting his fingers curl. Now it will begin.

When he retraces his steps in the evening
I will present the child, Jezreel, they will play—

my small hopes wanted only to be his,
to pass the nothingness of girlhood
to being a wife or woman's tuft of fire.

But I have heard him tell of the place, Jezreel,
the nauseous slant of light on its stones
and the evil of Jehu's rule. Isn't it wrong
to charge a child with the past? The girl
he named Lo-ruhama, "Not Loved," his second
son, Lo-ammi, "Not My People." We are less

his flesh than Israel. All that I have,
these children sweetened by roots, small,
are counters in a mind that holds hostages.
Yes, we are a nation, and like his, lost.

4.

A husband has no rivals. The first one,
not yet seventeen, crossed the stream
trailing lines of water, or he was
the second, out of breath and couldn't pour
fast enough, the water glazing his thin beard,

spilling down both sides of his face
leading him in. Whichever he was,
he was the first, awkward
as the orphaned lamb we kept staked
near the house. I soothed them

from their clothes, unsure, with eyes
you could pour alternatives into
and tufts of arrogant hair under their arms,

strong impatient lovers. I'm afraid
to say how long it took
to find men who teased the writhing out,
but the boys were mouth to mouth, I
not much older. They seemed brothers

and never stopped to think before they smashed
my clay pots. Hosea's bed, his house,
the children growing . . . I feed

and pull a dress over the girl's head,
scrub the faces of the boys
wriggling like a vine's tendrils
to bear their own weight. Leah and Shashona

and Debora come to mind, how we bathed
and inspected in the years
at my father's. I do what I'm told, but someone
must tell me I'm his or I hear Hosea.

5.

Hosea's superior voice didn't come to my room.
The night he brought me back, he prowled
the gateposts while my tossing knotted the sheets.
They will gnash their teeth, which He
has set on edge. So I was nothing

again, a common brown cup tied to the wall
for travelers. Standing on the market steps
as the scales idled and nuts were mounded—
in the gutter, the juicelss pulp of an orange—
merchants, soldiers, he stopped them all

shouting what they brought down on their heads.
When he left they clumped for a moment
before fear ran into anger. In markets, ports,

wherever ten people gathered, his thunder
gathered. And then one unmarkable day
the voice that had guided him
stopped. His frequent silences brushed
the heads of the children; I was
the proof of a farm's handiwork. Men think

we feel them grown in us, that before they spit
they fill us. Maybe, and maybe we just close
around them. Even if I cared to
I couldn't touch him, though this spring
the wind has dried my sweat.

Oh, I am prudent enough
to keep the rest dark, and as long
as possible.

Four

OUR GENEALOGY

The crickets scrape away
their tune, the evening's
temperature, as he props
both elbows. He plans to get rich
soon, and not by working
on the railroad. A half-moon
climbs chokecherry, willow,
and he tells me, *when the price*
of gasoline gets high
enough, there'll be plenty.

Who will he count with
when he fails, when he has to
blame the nameless faces
of bad luck, his genealogy?
A murderous Reich stripped
first names from its Jews;
it called them all
Sarah and *Israel.* Before that
outlanders and peasants
had no family names. A Kaiser

decreed them. X the son of
Y, X of Riga, X the tailor,
lumberman, drayman or
hapless fool: how they bore
those names like their own
bodies to other shores
until an immigration clerk got
something wrong or a new job
required something shorter.
Our fathers and mothers pointed

each time they cried *child*,
as the Jew does, repeatedly
insisting, *we Jews*. There are
histories one has to brush
against the grain to bare.
The crickets rub them tonight,
the ever-hopeful rich too, pausing
to lock their gas tanks;
and pale blue ridges whose
itching recalls the parted

flesh. My friend unfolds
his arms, his iron sights
on the future and his elbows
separating past from soft-ashed
past, between the crickets' legs,
the chill. *Only the orphaned
temporarily shiver these days*,
he says as he hugs himself,
his arms barely crossing
his chest like thin covers.

His unspoken questions relate to unhappiness
less than footing and grasp of self, the shuffle
that sends him past solid you. At the window
he points: a break in the haze, a house he lived in.

Such exiles resemble each other as they pass
without sharp contours into the future. Having
failed to allow for ice-glazed cobblestones,
their own forcefulness continues them past

any objective. He has uncovered the places he missed
which confirms this one, a reversed birth of
the self, the enactment as graceless, he says,
as sadness is, or aging where it affects the skin,

esse, he insists, more the product of friction
than *percipi* and the fog that wraps the years.
Dissembling, he hopes for a gate, beyond: a lake
in which the bottomless sky is turned and reflected.

Time knits its sweaters
of fog in such bones
as these branches. Today,
in translation, we repeat
the Russian trees: birch,
fir, pine—our convergent
landscapes—while the angels
in the snow flutter Osip.

When we vowed to become
lighter than air, at least
saints, our index fingers
pointing to axes and apples,
other quotidian dependencies,
did we suspect the pure,
that their sort cultivate
an almost metallic spite?

Come, stare through the trees
at the ice blue lozenges
of heaven, the white wisps
that misted your canals
and wide boulevards. Hook
and clasp, they fasten
passing quickly on. These
tired days, we drag you along

inventing further improbable
tours of exasperation. The clouds
must remind you of an ending,
your *wooden casket* (Moscow),
nowhere one can run, not Petrograd,
Petropolis, and the China blue
sky—bright eternally!—
the snow smelling of apples.

The small woman breathing next to him stirs,
and another, taller, is lightly covered.
Neither woman is his, not the one sleeping

in the dark room nor the other the lights bring
when a lattice skims the wall. Sleep will not have him
nor the two women, close, both beautiful,

rustling when he falls between them. An hour, two hours—
he wants it to be dawn, but there's a question
he has to turn over, he has to turn over and over.

MUSHROOMS

The clerk only worked and kept a room there
for disappointments. He would register them

then turn back to his reading. Madeline
and Rhea were a fairy ring of mushrooms

on his parents' lawn. From the topmost stair
someone called and he reentered childhood,

sliding beneath the covers where she let him
inspect, the crisp sheets and afternoons

never bright enough to guide a lost one
from the forest. Now lakes, reflections

on the alley window. Do they accuse him
of having shrunk into a suit and soft chair?

Upstairs a woman strips, a bellboy stoops
sighing by the vacant keyhole. At his desk

the clerk opens a book and the sagging hotel
takes a deep breath: pools of stagnant water—

always a body rising out of dim intransigence.

A SECRET

He wanted to tell her about the flashlight
picking a way among the boulders
as the two of them had on a beach, water
rushing toward them, a flight
of honkers across the twin spiked moon

just like a September calendar. But
they crossed only in long letters. These changed
the narrow mattresses and overcooked food
into a form of nostalgia he had managed
to stop writing down. It was no good

courting the fatuous past when
so many women from the back resembled her.
He returned to his room; it was clean
and self-chosen. He constructed the details
to a secret in case they ever met again

which he suspected they would not, a charm
like her name that he would leave unsaid.

gave himself permission to turn away
from the trees sparkling as this leaf
or that took light. He seemed to gather
the hills and bees indiscriminately
with ducks and rattlers, carrying them
as a child's toys to a hamper.

There was the acrid taste of woodsmoke,
certain birds crying out or the mice
in their talons. With the world dimmed,
falling with the sun past a ledge
he might have welcomed that clearing,
as of a stage, the shorn perspective,

had he loved himself more. He might have
missed that plentitude and, sighing,
relished his regret. But his eyes
found remarkably little, and that bound
text to page: black branches joining
a black sky—open and shut. Others lay

their bodies down, slow ed the breath
and roll of their flesh through space.
Others dreamt messages stalked them
and a terrible fear shook someone
bolt upright in bed, sometimes screaming.
Nothing like that with his sunrise.

At noon's repeated approach his feet
tangled between a chair and open door.
When the phone rang through his rooms
he ground extended ovals in the rug.
And his car wandered over the road:
headaches, sour breath—a mirror

of faces he could almost reach through
exploding into murky breath. He came
to long for the death of an old friend,
no one in particular, but a connection
to mull over, a light he might mourn
and recall with rare, unexpected warmth.

He lifts his head to check
she has not moved as she looks
across the room to him. It's time
to stop at the door, to kiss and wish
each other well. No one can know
of more between them than the salt air
that carries off their separate longings.

The icy stars stare overhead.
A steep street rises before them.
A lighthouse beam that froze them once
sweeps each singly. Claw of a pine,
line of a distant coast or clouds
that stretch along the strait. Time's arrow
can only point its one tyrannous way.

DIVIDED LOYALTIES

The cold fixed stars—walking with them
you sense a brittleness as they turn

hour by hour, above and within. A breeze
skims the grasses, the paths you take

habitually. At night you court
such loneliness it seems suspended

and the ten thousand thousand coarse grains,
salt drilling in ice. Your loyalties

divide then, weight for weight, white
bones to exchange as the stars blink on.

You could believe yourself their one-and-only
if only they didn't blink off too.

HER CHANGING

Soon the monthly floods
on which she floated free—
which ebb—will cease, and she
bear one unchanging mood.

She cries, still beautiful
beyond his reach. His body
knows of gravity
and years, their downward pull,

cold comfort and shrouding.
The moon's ring could sail
over a ridge to fill
his bowels with only longing—

and her mentioning it imply
a desire to exclude him.
Neither speaks. She swims
full and dark with the tides

as he watches the glaze
of her eyes. They recall birds
rocking on waves, the words
and worlds that look both ways.

BETRAYALS

In rooms in Moscow a party goes on.
As snow leans against the steps
a woman's husky voice moves through
the folksong of wolves, a troika
and snow. Everyone wears a fur coat—
all that body heat and it's still frigid.
Pasternak is reciting. He points
to the woman singer, his gesture
containing a possible threat,

and at once withdraws the hand
that no one, least of all she, mistake
his intent. The troika skims the snow,
the wolves far off or as yet unnoticed.
You must imagine the song continues
as the guests strain at Pasternak's words
into the phone, meek and pale, that
the room quiets as if Stalin filled it
and he has only called an expert,

the suave Pasternak, who responds
quite properly. This is the terror, these
the terrorized. You must remember
Mandelstam, so uncompromising
even his attempts to bend seem stiff,
has been temporarily saved. The snow,
which no one would trust weariness to,
has many more right things to do
than Pasternak, accomplishing his

impurely. Your attention is indiscrete.
Be sorry—the snow is. How pleasant
it would be to return to the party
at this point, some vodka, sardines,
blackbread—and forget. The troika
would very much like to outrun
the wolves. In the folksong, lights
from a town would swim into view
fueling one last galloping hope.

AUTUMN

The lambs are to market, the cattle will be culled
and the maples seem all trunk, switch or bone
and loose ends. Who wouldn't join them, hone
the edge of himself and let go: fall curled

and clacking—or, refined, leaving off
the stink of memory's mean bookkeeping. *I offer*
my first unborn child; that old man, my father;
a niece and nephews to the flames; my youth.

As if they hadn't been taken and I were more
than hide to strop a blade on, my close shave
the one I begged for, gorging on desire.

The markets claim their lambs each fall. I'd starve
for meat to cut and chew, my sweet and sour
portion, but for the heart's muscle, love.

Mark Halperin attended public schools in New York, where he was born, and graduated from Bard College with a B.A. in physics. He subsequently worked as a junior research physicist, travelled, studied philosophy, and worked as an electron microscope technician.

After receiving an M.F.A. in poetry from the University of Iowa, he moved to Ellensburg in 1966 and has taught there at Central Washington University ever since, with the exception of a year at the University of Arizona and a sabbatical leave spent largely in Mexico.

The University of Pittsburgh Press published his first book of poems, *BACKROADS*. Since then, Jawbone Press has published a chapbook, *The White Coverlet*, and Sea Pen Press issued a limited edition of the long poem, *Gomer*.

Halperin lives in the country near the Yakima River with his wife, Barbara, and son, Noah.

A NOTE ON THE TYPE

The text is set in 10 point Trump Mediaeval, designed by Georg Trump in 1954. Palatino italic, designed by Hermann Zapf, is used for display. Type set by Irish Setter in Portland.